Photo: Martin Hayward Smith

AN AFFAIR WITH RED SQUIRRELS

SQUIRREL

Your first glimpse
Is a gasp –

Easily
The finest breath of your life.

You appeal

To the colour of a sunken sun
Alive in a late beech hedge, glowing
Copper coins, sandstone
Crumbling through your fingers,
To confirm this home-hearth warmth
That widens your eyes even more

With a size
You didn't expect – so tiny
Yet of course it's how you'd
Fit a tangled woodland
Top to bottom
Like a hand in glove.

Straightaway you want to touch,
To feel her roundly sit-up back.
Straightaway
You can't – your Squirrel suddenly rusts
The length of a branch
With a soft blaze, a very
Light-fingered fizz.

Stuart Medland

A victim of squirrel mania

An Affair with Red Squirrels

DAVID STAPLEFORD

Member of the National Red Squirrel Captive Breeding Programme,
(East Anglian Branch)

*This book is dedicated to my father-in-law, Reg Owen
who generously allowed me to use part of his beloved garden
to build my first enclosure.*

Photography by Martin Hayward Smith
and the author

Poems by Stuart Medland

Larks Press

Published by the Larks Press
Ordnance Farmhouse, Guist Bottom, Dereham NR20 5PF

E-mail: Larks.Press@btinternet.com
Website:www.booksatlarkspress.co.uk
01328 829207

Printed at the Lanceni Press,
Garrood Drive, Fakenham

First printed February 2003

British Library Cataloguing-in-Publication Data
A catalogue record for this book is available
from the British Library

ACKNOWLEDGEMENTS

There are many people not mentioned in the text of this book who have given support and encouragement which has helped to sustain my work. They all share a love of red squirrels, but most are less eccentric than the author. I am probably most indebted to my wife who has tolerated my 'affair' and at times given crucial help, not least when I was at school, and, on occasion, she had to juggle the baby's bottle in one hand and the squirrel's pipette in the other.

My thanks are due to those field workers I disturbed by calling their mobile phones when they were up trees, in the middle of swamps or tracking the signal of a squirrel.

I am greatly indebted to Dr John Gurnell, Ian Robinson and Peter Lurz and Peter Dickinson who have shared their expertise and been of practical help during the lean times. I must also mention John Goldsmith and Geoff Fletcher for close backing, and also Helen Butler, Derek Gow, Bill Makins, Harry Pepper, Steve Downer, Janie Steele, Tim Venning, Jonathan Reynolds and Mike Jordan.

Thanks are due to the Norfolk Wildlife Trust (formerly the Norfolk Naturalists Trust) for permission to quote from Bird and Mammal reports. Last but not least, thanks to Susan Yaxley of the Larks Press who first suggested the book, cajoled me into writing it and hit upon the title, which is undoubtedly appropriate.

Introduction: Observations of a Nutcase

Some years ago in Fakenham, I gave a talk to a group of children from the Tud Valley Watch group in my garden. They came primarily to see the red squirrels, but also various other small mammals. The baby squirrels were in the nest at the time, so the group returned a few weeks later to see the young squirrels at play. On this occasion they presented me with a small, ancient suitcase to keep squirrel food in. On the side of the suitcase they printed in large letters NUTCASE and as I had been a victim of squirrel mania for thirty-six years I felt the title was very apt.

Instead of food, I keep various artefacts in the case as visual aids for when I give talks. Perhaps the most important of these is the pelt of a female red squirrel that had a very adventurous life including two notable escapes. However I use it as a first exhibit because it is a reminder of my initial interest in the red squirrel, arguably our most attractive mammal, which truly does 'grace the coniferous woodlands' as a native of Scotland once commented.

In 1940, at the age of six, I was evacuated to Headley in Hampshire from London. Each day I walked one-and-a-half miles to school in Kingsclere. I was in the middle infants' class and each afternoon the partition was rolled back and the top infant teacher spoke to both classes. On one occasion she was showing us the contents of her nature table and held up the body of a red squirrel. It was one of those magic moments that etch into the memory and that point in time is retained for me for life with great clarity. It was bright orange-red in colour and its elfin shape I can see now, clearer than a photograph. It was 1963, twenty-three years later, before I saw my first live red squirrel, in Thetford Forest. In 1963 red squirrels were plentiful in the Forest and one Saturday afternoon walking through the rides I counted 22 red squirrels and had a close view of all of them. That was almost as gratifying as that event in 1940 when a flame was lit for me that has burned brightly ever since.

Even now, after observing the behaviour of red squirrels at close quarters for thirty-six years, I feel I am still scratching the surface of knowledge about them.

How observant are we of the wildlife around us? On one occasion on an early morning walk in Shanklin, Isle of Wight, I was hoping for a sighting of red squirrels; there were no greys on the island. I met an elderly lady walking in the opposite direction towards town. I asked her if she had seen any red squirrels in the area. Her reply was, 'I know they are about on the Island but I've never seen one. I have done this walk every day for nineteen years to buy my daily newspaper and I've never

1

Farmer John Barnett on the occasion of my first sighting of red squirrels in Thetford Forest in 1963

seen a squirrel.' Twenty metres away from this spot, I noticed some freshly shredded pine cones on the ground beneath a high wall. I positioned myself there for five minutes and sure enough a red squirrel came bounding along the wall and reached up to the pine branches and proceeded to strip the cones and eat the seeds. The pine cones falling to the ground could be clearly heard. After ten minutes the lady returned with her paper under her arm. Should I tell her about the squirrel or watch to see if she would notice? I chose the latter course and she hurried by without noticing the squirrel above her head, feeding happily. If I had run after her the squirrel would have gone and she did not glance across the lane to where I was standing to catch my eye.

I remember this occasion with a wry smile when apparently authoritative statements are made about squirrels. For instance 'red squirrels do not eat sweet chestnuts, therefore they are at a disadvantage to greys', - this was reported in a broadsheet newspaper. In fact, in late October when the sweet chestnuts ripen, my red squirrels demolish them in preference to all else. 'Red squirrels are dying out because they can't digest acorns' ran the headline. Yet my reds love acorns when they are green and I have noticed that greys seem to prefer them at this stage as well. On that day in 1963 when I counted twenty-two red squirrels, five of them were feeding together in one oak tree, on the abundant green acorns it carried.

Red squirrel feeding on haws and green acorns

When man interferes, the natural balance is often upset and the red squirrel/grey squirrel saga is a simple example. The introduction to this island of the grey squirrel from the United States began in 1876, and set a ball rolling that seems now to be unstoppable. The first lines of Sir John Betjeman's auto-biographical poem *Summoned by Bells,* published in 1954, begins,

'Here on the southern slopes of Highgate Hill red squirrels leap the hornbeams.' That first chapter is titled 'Before MCMXIV', and certainly before 1914 it would have been reds that inhabited Highgate. Now of course it is grey squirrels that leap the hornbeams and it seems likely to remain that way.

I have a cousin who enjoys trawling through second-hand bookshops and he occasionally passes on little treasures that he comes across. One book he found for me is *How I tamed the Wild Squirrels* by Eleanor Tyrrel. The book was printed before 1919, and not once in the book is the colour of the squirrels mentioned, because there was only one sort of squirrel around in that county at that time and its colour was red. In the 1990s I bought a book about Hurtwood, Surrey, and squirrels were mentioned in it, but never at any time was their colour referred to. This is because there were only greys and the reds had long since gone. So much for the comment by Watt in 1923: 'I am of [the] opinion that the grey squirrel can never become wide-spread and dominant like our other introduced animals, the rabbit and the brown rat.'

I moved to Norfolk in 1979 and grey squirrels were colonising the county from the south and west. We moved in on 31st July and the previous owner of the house visited us from her new home in Wells-next-the-Sea. When she arrived, she excitedly announced that she had seen a young red squirrel cross the road at Waterden cross-roads. Over the next few days I made several visits to the pine woods at Wells in the early morning and on each occasion I was able to watch the red squirrels feeding in the tops of the pines, with the dog-walkers moving smartly along below quite unaware of the charming view above. Some weeks later, I found the first dead body, clearly marked with lesions that I later learned were caused by the dreaded parapox virus. From this time on the red rapidly disappeared in North Norfolk; greys were increasingly reported. Between Hillington and King's Lynn the road dissects some woodland and at one end was the body of a grey killed on the road; the casualty at the other end was a red.

I frequently inquired as to the presence of red squirrels and a clear pattern emerged. 'Yes there are red squirrels,' on the golf course, in the local wood, even seen in the garden. Then the observer would see me a fortnight later and comment that since my question they had looked particularly and there were no squirrels to be seen and several reported seeing a single grey.

One of the remaining outposts of the red squirrel in England is at Formby, on the Lancashire coast between Liverpool and Southport. Here, there is a substantial area of pine woodland, similar to that at Wells-next-the-Sea but more extensive, and the red squirrel flourishes with no competition from grey at present. George Bilsboro at one time reared many orphans and gained experience with grey as well. I remember him commenting 'the grey is built for survival,' and it seems to be determined to succeed at all costs. It breeds more frequently and has more young, on average, in a litter. The comment by one English Nature observer that it is 'oversexed, overfed and over here' seems entirely appropriate.

Most of us will have witnessed many of them in our parks, abounding in numbers, tackling discarded sandwiches and raiding litter bins, their bulky, sometimes fat appearance contrasting noticeably with the slimmer red. This again enables it to survive the lean times better. They are frequently twice the weight of the red. Mammals Trust UK gives the weight of the red as 250-300 grams as opposed to 400-600 grams for the grey. Some continental red squirrels that are presently being imported can be noticeably heavier than those found in Britain, sometimes weighing in at 350 grams, still far lighter than the grey.

1. The Coming of the Greys

Historically the red squirrel was widespread over the whole of the British Isles, arriving after the end of the last Ice Age. Although it suffered periodic fluctuations through disease, it was man's impact with deforestation that has altered the status and distribution of the red squirrel. The beginning of the 19th century saw tree-planting on a large scale, especially of fast-growing conifers and by 1900 the red squirrel had reached peak numbers. The story and subsequent decline after this point is intimately linked with the arrival of the grey squirrel from the USA in the late nineteenth century. Apart from the key introduction at Woburn, Bedfordshire, of ten grey squirrels in 1890 there were thirty-three known introductions, well documented, in the next thirty years and only one failed. The grey squirrel is reliably reported as spreading at the rate of six miles a year.

Though the red squirrel clearly shows a preference for coniferous woodland, before the advent of the grey squirrel it was well represented in our deciduous woodland and many people fondly remember its presence in London parks and areas such as Epping Forest.

Browsing one day in a second-hand bookshop I noticed the sketch of a grey squirrel on the dust-jacket of a book entitled *The Waters under the Earth* by John Moore. The first page begins 'Saw red squirrel. Rare as the dodo now!' This was an entry in a diary, the date of which was 31st July 1939, and the disappearance of the red had coincided with the arrival of the grey squirrels. The county was Gloucestershire.

A paragraph from the last chapter in the book is worth quoting:-

'You cheeky little upstart, thought Ferdo, ousting your betters, those beautiful bright red squirrels, from my Doddington woods! They've lived here since long before the Domesday Book. Nobody in these parts had heard of your kind thirty years ago...'

A few pages on, in the last paragraph of the book, Ferdo's thoughts have changed significantly and it reads, 'His grey squirrel came hopping out of the darkness and perkily appeared on the lawn. Taking a good look round, it sat up on its hind legs and surveyed its world.'

Many people will have a fleeting regret, if they remember at all, that the alien grey has supplanted the native red, but a squirrel is a squirrel and they would prefer to have a grey on their lawn or bird table than none at all. Its regrettable habits of raiding nest boxes for eggs or nestlings, digging up precious flower buds, wastefully plundering whole hazel nut crops before they are ripe, and decimating strawberry beds, are overlooked because of its charming antics, so it is tolerated and often encouraged with supplementary feeding.

Two predators on red squirrels, the goshawk and the wildcat

Photos: Martin Hayward Smith

A wildcat at Shanklin Chine in the Isle of Wight once demolished the whole local population of red squirrels

Goshawk feeding on red squirrel. They have been known to feed their young on twelve red squirrels– a day.

Of course this does not include those who have directly suffered more crucial damage, like the friend of mine who paid out £300 to repair the damage done to his loft by five grey squirrels, which were subsequently trapped, or another friend, who in order to avoid a similar bill had fifteen greys trapped in his loft over one winter. I do know they would not have received protests by animal rights activists too kindly.

I have a colour print of a grey squirrel in typical feeding pose sitting on a park bench eating a peanut. This is a good illustration of the fact that the grey squirrel is actively encouraged, and has flourished ever since its release. It is no exaggeration to call it ubiquitous in England and Wales and parts of Scotland. It had few natural predators with pine martens and goshawks rare or absent, and the ten squirrels released at Woburn clearly found conditions so much to their liking that they increased rapidly. This group was used to stock several other introductions, and the most successful invasion since the Norman Conquest had begun. Gilbert White's innocent comment in 1789, that 'The quadrupeds of Britain are so few that every new species is a great acquisition', takes on a very different complexion now. It contrasts sharply with Michael Meacher's words at the launch of the Mammals Trust U.K., that 'introductions have caused more extinctions than any other factor'.

I took several groups of pupils to an excellent campsite in Cuffley, Hertfordshire, and the warden always stressed that tents had to be laced up and all food put away in tins. Despite his warnings, many a boy or girl reported the cake or sweets they had been sent had been eaten by the voracious grey squirrels that abounded on site. Unfortunately they breed twice a year whereas the red often has only one annual litter. Their litters are also larger, often numbering five or six kittens.

As the grey increased and spread in central England, so red squirrels disappeared from those areas. Maps of 1920 and 1930 show clearly the spread of the grey and the comparative maps of 1940 and 1984 are graphic indications of grey expansion and red retreat. Perhaps the strongest indication of this is in Poole Harbour, Dorset. Here the grey squirrel inhabits all the mainland area even on the Sandbanks peninsula, having traversed the connecting road which appears to be a barren highway for squirrels, but since the grey is said to spend seventy per cent of its life on the ground perhaps this is hardly surprising, and they have been found traversing moors where there is no tree in sight. One was found in a coypu trap in a tiny island in the middle of a Norfolk Broad. This report gained credibility when my friend Kevin Hart reported seeing a grey swimming some hundred metres across a stretch of water on the Broads. He said its tail was extended above the water and it seemed so self-assured that he felt it was on a regular route.

For many years it was claimed that the grey did not displace the red, but merely invaded empty territory vacated by it. Then, as the grey flooded the area, the red could not win back a foothold. However, the Three islands in Poole Harbour tell a different story as Brownsea has a fairly stable population of around two hundred red, Fursey some forty squirrels and Green Island around fifteen. Before the red squirrels of Cannock Chase died out as greys took over, someone had the foresight to transfer a pair to Fursey. This pair soon bred and caused an increase to its present population. Whether the reds on Green Island were introduced or swam the narrow stretch of water is uncertain.

The other main island population of red squirrels, apart from Arran in Scotland, is on the Isle of Wight, where the red squirrels were said to number some fifteen hundred. Fortunately this population is well managed and encouraged. Helen Butler has done some wonderful pioneer work in this respect and her study document, aptly entitled 'Corridors of Hope,' alerted many to the importance of the Isle of Wight population and the need to plant trees and hedgerows, rather than felling and grubbing out, to bolster the squirrel numbers. Helen's efforts seem to be bearing good fruit because I note in a recent bulletin that the Wight population was estimated at three thousand.

One most interesting outpost of red squirrels in England is at Formby, on the Lancashire coast, north of Liverpool. Here in the pines, red squirrels abound. It seems likely that these are descended from some continental reds released there in the 1920s.

This apart, the red continues to decline, sometimes dramatically with the parapox virus, which often seems to appear after the arrival of the greys. This virus is as devastating to the red squirrel as myxomatosis to rabbits, probably more so, as rabbits seem to bounce back.

So, do we let nature take its course and just observe as our native red squirrel goes the way of the dodo? Or do we make an effort to redress the balance or at least do something to try and preserve this beautiful creature? The comment of an Alaskan scientist on global warming really struck a chord with me when he said, 'I have to do something, because I don't want to say to my grandchild, "Here's the earth. Here's what I've done to it. I've kind of messed it up for you."' I feel the same with regard to the red squirrel. I have a stuffed specimen given to me by a farmer from Gateley, in Norfolk. It was killed on the road in that very rural area, so reds were probably plentiful at the time. I don't want to be reduced to saying to my grandchild 'I'd like to tell you about an incredibly beautiful animal; here's the best I can do to show you what it was like.'

Cumbria, until recently, has been a stronghold of the reds, but greys are now making significant inroads into the county. The situation in Northumberland is similar. In Scotland, for some time now, it has been estimated that there are 200,000 greys and 120,000 reds though I suspect by now the respective numbers have increased for grey and declined for red if previous trends are anything to go by. When I spoke to a wildlife warden he said the grey had been moving north up the A9 and had reached Pitlochry. He hoped the Great Glen would be a natural barrier.

Glocænog Forest in North Wales still supports a population of reds and efforts are being made to conserve it, while Anglesey presents an extremely interesting picture. It was a stronghold for the red squirrel but greys crossed the Menai Straits, probably via the road or rail bridges, but some have certainly been known to swim across as there have been at least two specific eyewitness accounts. As a result of the grey incursion, the population of red dwindled to a small number in the south-east of the island around Pentræth Forest. At this eleventh hour an initiative was launched to eliminate or at least control the grey and as a result the population around Pentræth has grown to around one hundred.

This was reported on Radio 4 and caused a furore with animal rights activists who have taken up cudgels, verbally at present, on behalf of the grey, saying it is being victimised unfairly as an alien. They have ranged themselves in opposition to the conservationists. Thus the controversy as to whether to redress the balance we have upset, or let nature take its own course, is now epitomised in Anglesey. Andrew Tyler, the director of the charity Animal Aid, said, 'This is an obscene and pointless cull. The grey squirrel is being killed for no other reason than that it is grey and foreign.' I find it illogical that activists campaign on behalf of the invader while ignoring the plight of the indigenous species.

A glance across to the continent of Europe is probably worth-while at this point as the red squirrel is found throughout wooded areas of Eurasia from the tree-line south to the Mediterranean coast, from Ireland in the west to Japan in the east.

At present Italy is the only country in continental Europe that contains populations of American grey squirrels (*Sciuris cardinensis*). Two pairs were introduced into Piedmont (north-west Italy) in 1948. In 1966, five squirrels were released at Genoa Nervi, and in 1994 three pairs were released at Trecate, but these were recaptured two years later. At Genoa Nervi, the site is surrounded by sea and busy roads, and expansion is thought to be unlikely.

The Piedmont population has shown a rapid increase in recent decades, and in 1999 was said to be present in an area of 880 square kilometres (Bertolino, Genovesi). Eradication is now thought to be impracticable. A trial eradication was started in May 1997, but the project was opposed by animal rights groups and the resulting court action caused a three-year suspension of activity which allowed a significant expansion of the grey squirrel's range. As it has spread, the red has retreated and, apart from this major threat to its survival, the future impact on forests and commercial tree plantation would seem to be regrettable.

9

2. Beginnings

In 1999 I had the good fortune to spend three days in Wareham, Dorset with the European Squirrel Group. The highlight of the visit was a trip to Fursey Island in Poole Harbour, to see the red squirrels, those that were descended from the Cannock Chase pair. The island is covered with pine trees, which screen an oil well owned by B.P. After that introduction of one pair, the population, with no natural predators, exploded to a stable number of around forty squirrels.

Over the course of the three days some lectures with very impressive titles were presented, so when I was asked at the last minute to contribute I felt my title ought perhaps to be: 'Spatial awareness of *Sciuris Vulgaris leucourus Kerr* in highly concentrated suburban habitat: an attempt to combat parasite infestation causing heavy mortality and resultant decline,' or something similar. However, I opted for the more provocative 'The man who tried to breed red squirrels by purchasing two females!'

I was teaching my eleven-year-olds in 1964, in those nostalgic pre-National Curriculum days when teachers could choose their own inspired topic, and we were doing a class project on British Mammals. Brooke Bond tea had produced an album on British wild animals at the time and we were duly collecting the cards. On the cover was an eye-catching coloured sketch of a red squirrel and one of the girls, Lindsay Taylor, spotted this and said, 'In my weekly magazine *Cage and Aviary Birds* it advertises red squirrels costing £4 each.'

I immediately had visions of buying a pair, breeding them and releasing the progeny in the local woods - easy re-introduction, or so I thought. After all, naturalists were confidently stating at this time that the disappearance of the red had nothing whatever to do with the grey, so there should be no problem.

First I had to build the enclosure. I am not a D.I.Y. expert, but it's amazing what you can do if you have the incentive. Some hints were given on keeping squirrels in Monica Shorten's *Sunday Times* publication on red squirrels, so I used that as a guide. It recommended that the wooden frame be constructed outside the wire or the squirrels would gnaw through it. This may well be true of greys. Indeed a gamekeeper, seeing my apple tree inside the enclosure, commented, 'That would never survive with greys.' Be that as it may I never found the reds attacking the wood, so subsequent enclosures were constructed with the frame inside and this had the advantage of giving extra perches. I tried to simulate tree-tops inside the enclosure so there was plenty of 'furniture' for the squirrels to leap on, explore and establish their own territories.

I ordered my squirrels from Buntings of Buxton, Derbyshire, who had placed the advert in *Cage and Aviary Birds*. In my order I asked for 'a pair (male and female)' just in case 'pair' was not explicit enough. They duly arrived at New Barnet Railway station and I walked the two miles from my home to collect them. When I returned and released them from the plywood box into the enclosure they bolted into separate nest boxes and remained tucked away. One was a red-orange colour, almost certainly four years plus in age and the other a dark brown juvenile. As the dark brown one did not appear for two days, I coaxed it out of its box and found on closer inspection that it was in very poor condition with several claws missing and bleeding from the wounds. As it had been kept in close proximity with other squirrels, as a juvenile it would be a subordinate in the pecking order and had clearly been under severe stress as a result of the overcrowding in transit. Had it not been separated it would almost certainly have died. As it was, it recovered well and developed into a very good breeding female.

My first enclosure at Barnet. (My son Timothy shows the scale)

As the months passed, I was repeatedly asked if the squirrels had bred, and my stock answer was that they weren't in breeding condition. What I actually meant was that I couldn't see any evidence of a scrotum. Finally I decided to handle the squirrels to establish their sex, not an easy task as they were wild caught. I took them separately into the smallest room in the house, the toilet, where I could easily block off all bolt holes. Armed with a towel, using matador methods, I managed to catch them up and, covering their eyes with the towel, examined them at close quarters. They looked identical and I felt sure they were both female, which would certainly account for the absence of breeding behaviour.

I knew there was a large pet shop near Regent's Park Zoo, and as it seemed to have a wide variety of animals I called in one day and found it did indeed have imported red squirrels. I asked for a male and requested that I be shown the animal before I bought it. The proprietor put on a gauntlet with the comment that a bite was an unforgettable experience. He then plunged his hand into a cage that was no more than a metre cubed. In this cage were at least fourteen squirrels, which leapt in all directions as his hand entered sending a cloud of fleas up into the air. He managed to catch a squirrel, 'a male', and when he showed me, it clearly was! So much for my original 'pair'. When I related the story to him he just commented, 'Oh yes? I don't think he knows the difference.' (On several occasions pupils had reported to me that they had specifically asked for a male mouse, hamster or guinea pig, only to find it produced a litter of young shortly after purchase.) Having convinced me on this occasion of its sex, the shopkeeper placed the squirrel in what I can best describe as a small cake box. I then had to carry it on to the underground station at Camden Town. The tube train was full and I had to stand all the way to High Barnet, gingerly clutching my precious cake box. This proved to be too much of a stressful experience, because within two days the squirrel had died.

I had arrived home at dusk and there was a distinct chill in the March air. I tentatively opened the top of the box, but surprisingly the orange squirrel did not stir. I decided to allow it to emerge of its own accord and I tiptoed away. Certainly it was out the following day as its striking colour could clearly be seen from the house. However, it did not appear outside the nest-box on the second day, and when I decided to inspect the nest-box I found its inert body inside; clearly it had expired some hours previously. It looked in very good condition, but I did notice that the end of its tail had been bitten off, presumably in a fight. It might have been this, the trauma of the journey, or the sudden adverse turn in the weather that triggered fatal stress, or indeed a combination of all these factors.

I returned to the shop and haggled over the price of a new squirrel. He finally conceded ten shillings so I got a new male for £3 10s. I again had the cake-box experience, but I had learned one lesson. When I arrived home I turfed the squirrel out of the box and it immediately explored every nook and cranny of the enclosure and clearly felt quite at

12

home. This individual proved more vigorous, liked his new home, took to the juvenile female and breeding took place in the spring.

Having overcome the first hurdle, that of getting the squirrels to breed, the next, survival to maturity, proved even more difficult. The first litter numbered four but they all died shortly after weaning and subsequent litters of two and three suffered the same fate. On reflection they evidently died of stress as the enclosure was too small for more than three squirrels at most. The young squirrels developed roundworm, tapeworm or coccidiosis. Clearly too high a population caused stress, leading the squirrels to be run down and succumb to parasites and disease. At the time I didn't realise this and decided hand-rearing might be the answer. So I removed two of the three young of the next year's litter at twenty-eight days old, but before their eyes were due to open at thirty-one days. I fed them on ostermilk by means of an eyedropper. This way of feeding the young squirrels involved getting up hourly through the night to feed them in the first few days and later at less frequent intervals. I knew it was important to stimulate the young to defecate and urinate and this could be done by rubbing cotton wool dipped in a solution of water and antiseptic on to the genitalia. They were certainly regular as a result but they got very sore, and so I shared the rearing of the young with the mother and rotated them. This may have been unorthodox, but it worked very well although they were less tame as a result; they would take food from the hand and readily climb on me, but would not allow themselves to be handled.

Having ventured one attempt at hand-rearing, I resolved to try again when the next litter appeared. This time I removed a young male and fed him on lactol and glucose, which was a far more satisfactory diet. The lactol and various other tips were suggested to me by a young lad who helped to look after the animals at the small zoo at Verulamium, St Albans. I noticed among the exhibits there a baby grey squirrel some six weeks old and its teenage keeper told me precisely how he had hand-reared the orphan. I also came across some helpful suggestions in Graham Dangerfield's book *The Unintended Zoo*. As a result of this hand-rearing, this squirrel could be handled easily and even came when called. Perhaps a more detailed account of this behaviour will be of interest.

At this time at school I was reading a book to my class of first year juniors about a rabbit called Shadrach – not the most obvious name for a rabbit, but the story was a good one and Shadrach became an endearing personality to the pupils and to me, so it seemed right to name the squirrel Shadrach. This tamest of squirrels would disappear into a pocket in search of a nut, or indeed anything else that was worthy of attention. He would race around you excitedly, pleased at having found an extra tree trunk with bendable branches to negotiate, explore inside your sleeve to find a new and comfortable nest, inch his way up your back and ruin the collar of your shirt by puncturing the neat edging with his needle-sharp teeth. If he was feeling especially playful, he would curl up on his back in the palm of your hand and allow you to tickle him under the chin or on his white underside, while he playfully grasped your forefinger between paws or teeth, which gripped but did not bite. Occasionally on warm days he would sidle into the crook of your arm with his tail hanging limply down and close his eyes contentedly while he was stroked.

Shadrach enjoying a tickle

I had to spend more time with him than the other squirrels and in truth Nutty, his mother, was a little jealous. The only time I was bitten was an occasion when he was sitting feeding on my hand and she took a flying leap at him suddenly and attempted to bite; however, he leapt away and her bite missed him and landed on my finger instead. The teeth went straight through the cartilage and my finger bled profusely and was extremely painful - another lesson learnt.

Once breeding had began, I had the mistaken impression that you put two squirrels together, male and female, and that was it - breeding would necessarily follow. This has proved to be wrong. Even if everything else appears to be right, good food, plenty of space and right environment, breeding may not follow. The individual squirrels themselves are the crucial factor. A researcher on the continent stated that the best clue was to watch the individuals in infancy and note those that allowed touch, i.e. would allow another squirrel to approach and come in contact with it. When I lost my breeding male, further successful mating ceased, and after I had moved to Worcestershire my group of squirrels did not breed again although the enclosure was larger than the one in Barnet. Nutty, the female, had already produced litters,

14

but the males never showed any inclination to breed and I never noticed anything resembling a mating chase. A good-sized tree trunk (or perhaps several) in the squirrel enclosure can be very helpful as, in the mating chase, the squirrels seem to love pirouetting around them. In Malvern the main trunk in my enclosure was a mature cherry with a good girth, but the squirrels very rarely used it and I wonder whether the transverse bark of the cherry is not especially to their liking. My present enclosure includes the trunk of a mature oak, which is greatly loved by the squirrels, and I have seen many mating chases around it.

One potential hazard in seeing young animals through a crucial stage of development proved to be holidays. As a schoolteacher my annual family holiday was inevitably in August, just when late litters would be maturing. On two occasions my father-in-law was left in charge of feeding the squirrels and, although I left clear instructions, he deviated slightly from these in consecutive years. He was most well-meaning, but on my return I was alarmed when he said, 'I had an enormous crop of crab-apples and I gave a good number to the squirrels.' The adults wouldn't touch them of course, but the emerging young did, since it was natural for them to sample food put out for them. I found they had severe stomach problems as a result. The following year he had a surplus of white bread and thought the squirrels would benefit, again with unfortunate results.

After this I realised I had to leave the animals in the care of a naturalist who had a 'feel' for the wild. This proved to be a wise move, for on our next return from holiday I found a very flourishing menagerie. The squirrels were all fit and my dormice had multiplied dramatically. I remember sorting and sexing them with Stephen Harris (now Chairman of the Mammal Society and Professor of Environmental Sciences at Bristol University). We had them in my 'hospital' cage on the lounge table, and I recall his comment, 'dormouse tenement' as they were scattered over the wire, gripping tightly with their little feet.

As soon as I began keeping squirrels, people asked me what their names were. So, despite being immediately able to recognise them as individuals, I named them Rufty and Tufty. A school colleague raised her eyebrows and said 'Highly original!' but that did not deter me. Later, with regular yearly breeding in Norfolk, I gave the squirrels born in a particular year names beginning with successive letters of the alphabet. At the time of writing we have reached the letter O.

One of my Barnet squirrels I named Russ, perhaps an odd name for a squirrel, but among my pupils at the time was one lad who developed a keen interest in natural history. His name was Russell and he had bright red hair. One particular squirrel's coat was a strikingly similar colour, so it seemed right to name him Russ. Russell and I kept in touch for some years before his untimely death at a young age.

3. Malvern Days

In 1972 I was appointed Head of Malvern Parish C.E. primary school, Great Malvern, and that meant that the family had to leave East Barnet and move to Worcestershire, red squirrels and hazel dormice and all. When the removal day arrived every space in car and van was used up and the dormice had still not been loaded. There was no alternative but for me to return for them the following day. The squirrels' temporary cage had been trans-ported three days earlier. I had two *glis* (edible dormice) that I kept at school in an enclosure, large enough for *glis* but too small for squirrels. I realised it might do until I constructed a new enclosure of suitable size. So I gave the *glis* to a friend who worked in the Natural History Museum and hired a large van to transport the enclosure. With some hastily improvised carpentry and a little brute force I managed to squeeze it concertina-style into the van and took it to Malvern to deposit in the back garden ready for the arrival of the squirrels.

On the family moving day we transported the four squirrels, Shadrach, Nutty, Blackie and Russ in nest boxes in the car. They all arrived safely, but I realised that they could not happily survive together in the small cage. Nutty, Blackie and Russ would tolerate each other, but Shadrach was very much a humanised squirrel and the other three, especially Nutty, bullied him quite severely. As she was fairly tame herself, I believe she was jealous of Shadrach, hence the memorable bite she gave me.

Some people invite being bitten by advancing towards a squirrel with finger pointing straight at it. It concludes it is being offered a tasty morsel, so it sinks its teeth into this generous offering. My new neighbour in Malvern did just that and was most indignant when the squirrel drew blood with its needle-sharp teeth.

Since the squirrels were intolerant of Shadrach I removed him from the cage at night and kept him in the lobby adjoining the house. I found he was only content if I left my 'squirrel coat' in the lobby. This was the coat I had used when I had reared him and of course it was well chewed around the edges and the buttons were so well bitten as to be unrecognisable. On the third night I accidentally left the cage door open and in the morning the other three squirrels were gone! I placed food in the cage and left the door open. Nutty returned in a few hours and Russ by the evening. Blackie disappeared, but a neighbour 200 yards away reported seeing him in his garden. Unfortunately this meant he had crossed the road so I was not hopeful of his return, bearing in mind we had moved into a completely strange environment to the squirrels.

However, I set my trap in his back garden. I was delighted to hear my neighbour's distinctive, gruff Worcestershire voice again the following morning, but intrigued when he said 'There bain't no squirrel in your trap, but there's a mouse.' Realising it was a heavy treadle on that particular trap I thought it must be a yellowneck (*Apodemus flavicollis*) to be heavy enough to spring the trap. When I spied it, it certainly was a magnificent male yellowneck and I kept it for some months with two females I later trapped locally.

I never saw Blackie again; there was a possible sighting two years later at a Caravan Park two miles away. There was no possibility of confirming this for certain, but it did seem likely as I spoke to the lady concerned. She felt sure it was not a grey, and it came right into her hallway and leapt up on to one of the coats hanging from a peg. It hung there for a moment before leaping and disappearing out of the front door, not to be seen again.

I made my new enclosure within a fortnight and transferred the squirrels into it. Shadrach always exhibited slightly un-squirrel-like behaviour and two years after being in Malvern he apparently came out of his nest one very windy night and I found him dead on the floor of the enclosure next morning. Post mortem reports indicated death due to a severe crack on the head. I concluded that he was blown onto a branch in the high wind. Those who love animals will know how keenly I felt at this turn of events. He was five years old, which is a very good age for a red squirrel, but he could have survived for some years if he had been a little more cautious. He was a squirrel of great character and although each has a distinctive personality, like people, Shadrach was unique.

Breeding ceased when I left Barnet and the main benefit from the squirrels in Malvern was education, as they were a great attraction for visitors, friends and pupils. One of my school staff, Monica Woolley, Head of Infants, told me that she had noted the red squirrels in a local wood before going to college in the 1930s. The last sighting of a red squirrel in Malvern was 1953.

Shortly after my arrival in Worcestershire a retired Birmingham Head Teacher presented me with a beautiful drawing in coloured crayon of a 'School Creed'. Her school in Birmingham no longer existed and she asked me to hang the picture up in the hall at school. The relevance of this is that it was decorated on each side of the base with two beautifully drawn red squirrels, which were obviously the local squirrels native to Birmingham when the picture was produced in the 1920s. The picture was the only remaining artefact from her school. I accepted the gift with a certain reluctance. I had an immediate positive response to the values depicted in the words, but the illustrations around the border, of plants, animals and birds, though beautiful, were characteristic of a bygone age.

My temporary cage with the Malvern Hills in the background

During the second world war, many London children moved school at least once. I was five years old in 1939 and eleven in 1945 when the war ended, and during that time I attended six different primary schools. One thing common to all of them was that all the classrooms I entered had large wall-charts displayed, and their illustrations, even in the town schools, portrayed a rural idyll rather than an urban environment. The picture that the Birmingham Head gave me was hand-drawn by her art teacher in coloured crayon, but clearly reminiscent of those pre-second world war charts. One I remember in detail was of a young lady teacher walking through woodland and meeting a smartly-dressed young schoolboy who was raising his cap in greeting. The caption below read 'Good morning, Miss Dove.' It certainly got the message over to me at the time quite acceptably, but in post-war days it would have been laughable, as most pupils then would stuff their caps away in their satchels as soon as they were clear of the school gates. There in that woodland scene were the obligatory red squirrels peering down from the branches as if they too were saying 'Good morning, Miss Dove.'

When I moved on to Fakenham, Norfolk, in 1979 I felt the old-style format of the crayoned chart and perhaps some of the sentiments of the creed were too dated to transfer to a Junior school of the 1980s. I placed it by the dustbin. However Monica Woolley rescued it from such an ignominious end and parcelled it up and presented it back to me. So it did find its way to Fakenham after all and resided in my nature room for many years and the story behind it was related several times in school assembly. When I retired I changed my mind about the content being 'old hat' so I presented it to the school, written out in beautiful calligraphy by another teacher, Joan Norville.

18

Shadrach would agree to come into the porch –

After Shadrach's demise I realised I needed some new blood, and I thought the Lake District might be a likely source. In the hot dry summer of 1976 I borrowed a tent and paid a flying visit to Grange-in-Borrowdale where I camped by a swiftly-flowing brook which swept down from the mountainside. Here was a campsite where tents could be pitched. I had been tempted to come here by tales of many red squirrels visiting the site and foraging around the tents looking for food.

My long-suffering wife had given me two days' squirrel search and I was blessed in that time with excellent weather. The problem proved to be an almost complete absence of squirrels. However, I had one memorable sighting and anyone who has had a similar experience will empathise when I say that it was worth the trip for this alone.

– provided he could sleep in my squirrel coat

I was pondering over the events of a wonderful day, despite the fruitless search for squirrels or even signs of them, when I noticed a movement at the brow of the hill and the unmistakable shape of a red squirrel came bounding slowly towards me following the line of the brook. Every so often it would pause, stand up on its hind legs in that typical squirrel pose with its front paws across its chest, sniff the air for a moment and then proceed. When it came level with me, it bounded a few feet up a tree to nose and lick the moss on the bark, froze in still life for a second, then leapt to the ground, ran to the brook to lap at the swift- flowing water and, having taken its fill, proceeded down the hill and disappeared from view. It was quite absorbed in its own progress and was apparently quite unconcerned at my presence, though I could see that it was clearly aware of me and I am sure any movement on my part would have disturbed the magic of the moment.

Some years later, my friend Stuart Medland showed me some poems he had penned about red squirrels and this included the following poem on an encounter in Borrowdale. When I first read it the incident it related was so similar to my own it almost made the hairs on the back of my head stand out at the recollection of my own unforgettable experience. Stuart's pen had captured the spell far more vividly than I could and he has generously allowed me to include the poem here.

DERWENT WATER

A small brush fire
Suddenly sparked
From the conifer tinder

Across the path
Stopping halfway –
To juggle a cone

Like a shuttle on a loom
She throws her quick life
From one side to the other, one
Side to the other,

Leaping now –
Straight from sitting
To crackle dead wood
In the far-side trees, a skittering

Flare across what
No one told her
Was a fire-break gap

20

With the barely-a-sound
Of fingertips
On loose paper.

Now you are head-spinning party
To a chestnut romp, a skittering
Flicker of warm flame-fur leaving
Thin fur-smoke across your eyes – impossible

To follow round
And round again, while all the time
Binding you tighter and tighter
She pulls herself closer,

Until suddenly – bang –
She spreadeagles herself
Across the bark-face of an oak tree trunk
With a grip like crampons –

Holding your eye
With the oily bead of jet
Of her own.

I returned from the Lake District empty-handed, but the seed was
sown in my mind that I might be able at some point to use the
knowledge I had gained with my European reds by breeding some
indigenous red squirrels.

In 1977 there was much space taken up in the *West Midlands Press*
deploring the fact that Dudley Zoo was going to close and the animals
would be disposed of. At the time the zoo had one male red squirrel.
This was a hand-reared orphan, displayed in a prominent position as it
was very friendly and clearly a great attraction. I promptly visited the zoo
and asked to see the Curator and asked if there was a possibility of
obtaining the squirrel. He was sympathetic, but so pained at the likely
closure of the zoo that, understandably, getting rid of the squirrel was
not at the forefront of his mind.

Shortly after this, the zoo was given a reprieve and I am glad to say is
flourishing still and doing good work in the field of conservation. The
very satisfactory footnote to this little story is that precisely nineteen
years later, in 1996, Colin Hill, the keeper of small mammals at Dudley,
came to Fakenham to collect three of my Norfolk red squirrels to take
back to the West Midlands and incorporate them into the National
Captive Breeding Group.

In 1978 a nature exhibition was held at the Winter Gardens Hall in

Spreadeagled. Females love to lie flat in the sun when pregnant.

Photo: Martin Hayward Smith

Great Malvern and I was asked, together with a friend, Norman
Matthews, to assemble some small mammals for display. We set about
the task with Longworth traps and we also used my Legg traps for
squirrels to try and catch some water voles. The latter we set in a suitable vole run by the River Severn. As the Longworths were set in and
around a wood several miles from the Severn, Norman covered one
venue and I inspected the other site. The Longworths regularly caught
shrews, field voles, bank voles, wood mice and, excitingly, yellownecks,
but sadly there were no water voles in the Legg traps. Then one evening
I returned from the Leigh Sinton Wood to find an empty Legg trap on
my doorstep with the word MINK!!! printed in large letters.

Later, Norman gave me a graphic description of the scene that met
his eyes as he scrambled down the riverbank. More accurately it was the
sound he heard as he approached the river that caused alarm bells to
ring. He said the din was blood-curdling with the obscured animal
spitting and swearing (or the mink equivalent). He was certain that we
hadn't caught the mild-mannered water vole and his worst fears were
confirmed by the intimidating sight of the ferocious bundle of energy
that was hurling itself in frustration at the sides of the trap. Needless to
say, Norman realised the folly of attempting to display the mink in the
exhibition, so clearly he must let it go, but how? I remember him saying,
'No way was I going to get near that trap.' Ingeniously, he entered the
nearby spinney and fashioned a lengthy pole and managed gingerly to
lever the wire to lift the heavy metal plate, taking care that he did this
from the rear. The mink shot out of the trap and, much to Norman's
relief, straight into the Severn, where it disappeared from view. We
concluded after discussion that the family of water voles that were
previously in residence on that riverbank were no more, and
undoubtedly mink were the culprits, sadly an increasingly frequent
occurrence in our rivers.

We called it a day at this point with the water voles, but we had
assembled a good variety of small mammals, including of course the red

My 'hospital cage' housing three baby reds

squirrels. I displayed the squirrels in my 'hospital' cage, 3' × 18" × 18",and put some hay at one end for them to retreat into. The event was a full-day affair and was very well attended for the whole time. But it was clearly not a good experience for the two squirrels, Nutty and Russ. There were so many people that Norman and I were fielding detailed questions continuously and we were not able to give our full attention to preventing prodding fingers and attempts to get the squirrels to perform. Added to this was the aggravation of strong lighting and a constant hubbub of human voices; the squirrels must have been quite traumatised. It was a swift and salutary learning curve for me since within five days both had died. Russ was eight and a half and Nutty nine and a half.

Typical red squirrel pose

Photo given to the author

As they were both in good health at the time it is reasonable to assume they would have survived longer had I not put them through that trauma.

While in Malvern, I was invited to appear on a TV programme presented by Johnny Morris. The programme was called 'Women Only' and it went out live during the lunch hour. (I suppose in those days it was assumed that most men would then be at work, hence the title.) I was asked to go to Bristol for the programme and to take with me a variety of small mammals, including red squirrels, which were to be the main attraction. I agreed to appear and, in addition to squirrels and dormice I managed to trap some harvest mice, wood mice, yellownecks, bank voles and field voles. I took various aquariums for the mice and voles and my 'hospital cage' for the squirrels. I set up the presentation in the studio and waited...and waited. It was an hour and a half before the cameras were ready for a take. By that time, under the hot arc lights of the TV studio, the animals were all tucked away and sleeping soundly.

The plan was for Johnny Morris to walk the exhibits with me and ask suitable questions, 'Now what have we here?' etc. 'Never work with children or animals' the saying goes, and it certainly did not seem likely that I would get the small mammals to respond to the camera in these circumstances. However, I managed to obtain a long cane of the baton type and thought I would prod the mice and voles with it to encourage them to move at the appropriate time. The dormice would be fine because they would freeze. Amazingly, the plan worked well, but the squirrels were intended to be the climax and I remember I reached that point in a cold sweat. I took the precaution of having some hazel nuts in my pocket, more in hope than expectation. Sure enough, both squirrels were sound asleep in their nest-box. So, as I was answering Johnny's questions, I opened the cage and tilted the box, hoping one of the squirrels would come out, but not begin leaping all over the studio. Incredibly, Nutty emerged and sniffed at me. I produced a nut, which she promptly took, jumped on to the top of the box, and proceeded to gnaw in the traditional squirrel pose perfectly for the camera. I don't think the producer had any idea what a fortunate occurrence this was.

The particularly nerve-wracking ending was that Johnny's final question inevitably was, 'So then, why is it that red squirrels are on the retreat?' At that moment the TV man behind Johnny held up a notice in my direction, which said '30 seconds!' Any answer required at least five minutes. I can't recall how I coped with that one.

It had been a fascinating experience and the bonus was to have enjoyed the company of Johnny Morris in the canteen. He had a lovely easy manner and immediately joined us at table. He was a great raconteur and entertained us with accounts of extra-ordinary encounters he had had with animals and people over the years.

That period of time in Barnet and Malvern provided valuable experience for what lay ahead. We moved to Norfolk in 1979 and the scene was set for part two of the red squirrel story.

4. Norfolk

Ruth Race, in the HMSO booklet *East Anglian Forests*, gives a good summary of the squirrel situation in 1972:- 'Red squirrels are widely distributed and generally plentiful throughout the forest areas of Norfolk and Suffolk and specially so in conifer plantations...North American grey squirrels have been very slow in reaching East Anglia, in comparison with other parts of England. Some invaded south and south-west Suffolk between 1955 and 1960 and the population has rapidly increased.'

When greys did reach Thetford Forest they were aided in their advance by the corridors of deciduous trees and the deciduous amenity areas. (See Appendix: Greys and Reds in Essex)

In the mid-1980s I was invited to speak to a group of teen-agers in Norwich and one who lived in Newmarket Road said there were a pair of reds living in the trees at the rear of his garden whom the family virtually regarded as pets. Then greys appeared and the reds were no longer seen. The family investigated and found their dead bodies at the foot of the trees. Once again I asked the time lapse after the first grey was seen – 'Three weeks,' was the immediate reply. Elsewhere in Britain the process is sometimes reported as taking longer, sometimes years, but in Norfolk the changeover seems to have been dramatic. I have talked to many Norfolk people who have spoken fondly of the former plentiful presence of red squirrels in particular detail, but one reference to such times is worthy of specific mention. This came from Rosemary Tilbrook, one of a quartet of naturalists who wrote regularly for the *Eastern Daily Press* from 1986 onwards after the death of Ted Ellis. On 18th December 1986 she wrote a delightful article suitably entitled 'Paradise Lost'.

Memorably she recounted how she had viewed a cottage at Ashwellthorpe: 'The place was a dream of cow parsley and apple petals and there were red squirrels running along the gutters at the back of the cottage...No cottage was ever sold more quickly. For 20 years we lived in a fairy tale world of red squirrels.' Sacks of hard nuts were ordered to encourage them inside and outside the cottage. Rosemary's writing here was an eloquent indication of a situation mirrored in other parts of the county. The squirrels 'used to come down the chimneys at daybreak such was their enduring passion and impatience for nuts...Every morning I used to sit on a stool outside the kitchen door feeding as many as eight squirrels.' The name of the cottage was rightly changed to 'Red Squirrels' and 'Hognut and Company' were immortalised on the gate. But joy became grief... 'For they all caught a terrible disease, with discharging swollen noses and swollen eyes...and I fed them all by hand until they died.'

The red squirrel has ear tufts in winter (left) but not in summer (right). *Photos: Martin Hayward Smith*

It is not known for certain when grey squirrels first entered the county. Monica Shorten's book *Squirrels* in the New Naturalist series, published in 1954, suggested a possible early introduction at Felbrigg, which unusually did not establish. She also mentions a possible release in Suffolk. Early grey presence in low numbers often seemed to go unnoticed until an explosion in population took place.

The annual mammal reports of the Norfolk and Norwich Naturalists Society are a good guide as an indication of the grey/red situation in Norfolk and merit a closer inspection.

1963 Red: one of the most widespread of our mammals - the Thetford Forest population at this time estimated at several thousands. They were common as road casualties - always an indication of good numbers. Greys were noted in various locations on Norfolk boundaries, and someone made the comment, 'It's known that they travel in pairs for considerable distances through hedgerows.' Several instances of precise sightings of pairs moving in this manner were recorded. In November a pair was seen at Surlingham, one was shot at Wheatfen and another sighted in December.

1964 Red: reported from sites too numerous to mention. Nineteen road casualties were counted by one observer.

Grey: no certain reports. As in other counties - initial early reports of grey were followed by some years when it appeared to have gone to ground.

1965 Red: well distributed.

Grey: increasing in the Euston areas not very far over the border into Suffolk.

**The tail of the red squirrel, dark in winter on the left, will turn to
light champagne in summer**

1966 Red: particular reference to the thickly populated red squirrel area
of the Cringleford-Colney-Newmarket Road (Norwich) Triangle.
1967 Red: widespread
Grey: two reports - Ringland and Newmarket Road. One body produced
at the turn of the year.
1968 Red: well recorded. One observation here is worthy of note: 'in the
mixed woodland of Wheatfen they seem to have been absent for the first
time in more than twenty years - the only report of a decrease in the
county this year.' A glance back to 1963 will show that there were two
sightings of greys at Wheatfen in late 1963.
Grey: Now quite numerous in Suffolk. One at Quidenham in April
'shows their infiltration may now be under way'. One was shot by a
keeper at Aylmerton on June 26th - and this near Cromer.
1969 Red: reports were described as plentiful, although more than half
of these came from the Breckland forests.
Grey: reported a further considerable advance. It was hoped that the
fens to the west, the Breck pine forest and the Waveney would be
fortifications, but they have broken through in the south-west...
1970 Red: reports indicated that their numbers remain high though
there were a few indications of 'red squirrel disease' in parts of the
Brecks at the end of the year.
Grey: commented on the final establishment of the grey squirrel as a
regular breeding addition to the county fauna. The first pairs invaded in
1963 but their establishment had been more sudden and definite than
expected. Main means of infestation were south-west of Attleborough
and Thursford near Fakenham. Records were too numerous to detail.

1971 Red: large scale reduction in numbers by 'red squirrel disease' as it coincides with dramatic increase in grey squirrels - is the grey a 'carrier'? Animals found 'emaciated' only able to 'shuffle along.' It was interesting that in almost every case when- ever disease was reported within an isolated population, a grey squirrel was reported nearby either shortly before or afterwards. At Ashwellthorpe numbers visiting a garden reduced from 7 to 2 by disease. An interesting report here of one red squirrel swimming 20 feet to the other bank of the Wensum.
Grey: large scale spread. One turned up in a marshman's cottage garden near Reedham nearly a mile from the nearest trees and probably having swum several stretches of water to reach the site.
1972 Red: recorded as static. Good in North Norfolk - grey not well established.
Grey: much control tried; over 70 on one Breckland gibbet. One caught in an unbaited coypu trap at Wheatfen Broad.
1975 Red: regarding the Stamford Training Ground the following comment was made. 'The establishment of greys in the area coincided with the outbreak of 'red squirrel disease' and the 1969/70 peak was followed by a massive slump in red squirrel numbers.' The attempts at grey squirrel control are referred to, but these were counterbalanced by the double breeding season of the grey and its willingness to traverse open ground with very little cover.
1976 Red: Thetford Forest still holding out well, but 'elsewhere the news was less hopeful. Controllers of the grey found that any killed were quickly replaced by others moving in.
1977 Red: many contributors referred to fewer reds and more greys. 'Attempts to isolate the elusive virus responsible for 'red squirrel disease' continue.'
1978 The change from red to grey can be dramatically sudden. Until midsummer reds could be seen in Thorpe Woods and extensions even to the old City of Norwich but sightings then stopped and an ever-increasing number of greys were seen by large numbers of people.
1979 Apart from Thetford Forest the status of reds in the county was reported as 'uniformly depressing.' Despite widespread control, numbers of grey squirrels continue to increase. In the Stansted area, for example, there were more grey than red at their peak which points to the grey tolerating a higher density of population. In Thetford Forest greys appeared not to penetrate the large pine stands at first but stayed in the deciduous corridors.
1980 Reds were now so few outside the Forest that a sighting was a significant event. One estate reported killing over 1000 greys with no apparent reduction in their numbers.
1981 Red: rapid decline. The grey squirrel had more entries on the species index than any other mammal. This year included an article on

'Red and Grey' by Dr I. Keymer, Dr J. Reynolds and Mr J. Goldsmith.
1982 'Red and Grey' - an article by Dr J. C. Reynolds. Apart from the Thetford Forest population the only reports of red came from Shaker's Wood and parts of the Wensum Forest. Grey squirrels were observed to eat birds including bluetit, yellowhammer, greenfinch, blackbird and redwing.
1983 Red: nine contributors list sightings of remnant populations.
Grey: so numerous and widespread sightings go unrecorded.
1984 This report included Jonathan C. Reynolds insertion 'Squirrel Distribution in Norfolk',and his comment on the likely accuracy of red squirrel returns is worth quoting: 'In most cases where red squirrel populations appear to have disappeared since 1983, grey squirrels have been rcorded from the same 5 x 5 km grid square, implying that red squirrels had a good chance of being recorded if present.' The article went on to refer to apparent loss of reds at Holkham Meals, Lexham, Edgefield Woods, Blickling and Horsford Woods.
The general Rodentia report included the comment, 'Care must be taken not to mistake russet-backed greys for genuine reds.' I have noted that these mistakes are more commonly made in the years immediately following the disappearance of reds. Greys were referred to in the report as 'all over Norwich, even surmounting telegraph poles according to a press photograph'.
During this year I took a photograph myself of a young grey on a telegraph pole in my garden. I observed it for some time. It appeared to be surveying the terrain, i.e. the view from the top of the pole which poked out above the trees, by moving round 360 °. After sitting perched for some time, it climbed down and moved off in the direction of the nearest spinney.
1985 Dr I. Keymer reported that he had received no red squirrels during the year, alive or dead.
1986 Thetford population is widely scattered.
Grey: 'You name the location and they are there.' 'Our population is vast,' wrote one contributor who loves to watch them.
1987 Red: apart from Thetford one sighting at Wells Woods (one of my releases?).
Grey: entering roofs and lofts; devastation of young trees; robbing young birds and even adults from nest boxes.
1988 Red: none outside Thetford Forest.
Grey: reported taking sparrows from under roof tiles.

On arriving in Norfolk in 1979, we found that the red squirrel was fast disappearing, and as my son Timothy and I trawled the woods around Fakenham, searching in vain for positive signs, he said, 'If you don't do something about it, Dad, the red squirrel will be gone.' That jerked me into action and I asked several landowners if I could try to trap some squirrels in order to build up a group for potential release when the time was right.

I made my requests to the owners of woodlands where red squirrels had most recently been seen. Everywhere I asked, I received a positive response as long as I would use that location first in any future release. The fact that it took me twelve months to trap one pair and a further six months before I caught a second pair is an indication of how scarce the red had become in Norfolk in 1980. I would trap at a certain location until I was trapping grey squirrels or they were being regularly sighted, at which point I would move on to a new wood. In the course of this process the traps were sprung by various animals; songbirds, frogs, toads, hedgehogs and, of course, grey squirrels. Then one autumn evening I just had a feeling I should check the traps before morning and my young daughter said she'd like to come with me. I had two Legg traps and I had set one on the woodland floor under some Scots pines near a pile of recently stripped pine cones. As we approached the trap in the dappled sunlight beneath the pines, there was a red squirrel, clearly recently caught as it was moving vigorously in the trap and had only eaten half the bait. It was a male. Within thirty metres of this location I found a pine tree that was evidently being used on the regular route of a squirrel, as I could see the claw marks on the trunk, so I set the trap on a low branch. Two days later I caught a dark brown female there.

One North Norfolk man I approached regarding squirrels was George Cushing of Thursford and he had a most interesting tale to relate. He told me he used to walk his dog daily in his woods at Thursford and he expected to see red squirrels every day. He particularly mentioned one he saw daily and it seemed to greet him as he passed. One morning it fell dead in front of him, with no obvious wounds. He told me that reds disappeared within two months of his noting the first appearance of a grey.

At Thorpe, on the eastern side of Norwich, the comment of Tony Howes, a keen wildlife photographer, adds weight to this Thursford experience. He told me that red squirrels abounded in the Thorpe Woods and he was preparing for detailed work on photographing them, when he noticed a dramatic fall in numbers with several greys moving in. When he was ready to film there were no red squirrels left. He said the parapox virus was the cause. When I asked the question how long the process took he replied unhesitatingly, 'Six weeks.'

I had decided that I wouldn't build an enclosure before I caught any squirrels, but wait until my efforts proved successful. Fortunately we had a porch that ran the width of the house at the rear and my wife and I agreed that we would keep the squirrels there until I managed to build an enclosure in the garden. Thus we had the thrill of looking out from

A British red squirrel in summer moult, which works backwards from the head. The thicker winter fur can be seen on the squirrel's back.

A continental
squirrel
in Madrid,
large and dark
in colour
*Photo given to
the author*

31

our lounge window and seeing the two squirrels at close quarters for a few months, as my enclosure was not completed till spring time.

I believe I was amazingly fortunate to have picked one stretch of woodland where a few reds remained. This was a particularly interesting area as it consisted of a group of small woods separated by meadows, but linked by hedgerows. A forester commented later that he noticed that when grey squirrels arrived the reds moved on to another wood. I think I was lucky enough in my trapping to pick them up in this displacement. I tried to trap in other areas after this initial success, but after a few weeks I gave up. At that time Thurlow Craig used to write a weekly article for the *Sunday Express* and in the new year, after a sustained spell of very cold weather, he remarked that two emaciated grey squirrels had feebly struggled on to his bird table to feed on the bird food. This prompted me to try again and a hunch led me to set the trap in the wood where I had previously caught the two squirrels. Within three days I caught a pair. Thus I felt I had the nucleus of a breeding group. I released the four into my newly-built enclosure and hoped for breeding success.

I had built the enclosure around two old-established apple trees and the dimensions were 25 feet by 20 feet and 8 feet high. A chicken shed was within the enclosure and this gave the squirrels extra protection from the elements. In late summer both females produced litters of three young, but one deserted her nest.

I thought two pairs in such a large enclosure would be ideal, but the males proved very territorial and there was a clear pecking order, with one dominant and the other subordinate. The dominant would not allow the subordinate to emerge from the nest box and as the latter's condition deteriorated, I decided to release him. After I had released him, precisely in the spot where I had trapped him, I secured a nest box to a tree and put food out on a feeding platform. After some days the food was no longer taken, so I left him to his own devices.

I later released three more squirrels in the same wood, so I felt I had fulfilled my obligation and got a breeding group into the bargain. Was the red, spotted in Wells woods in 1987, one of those I had released, I wonder? I did my best to monitor the released squirrels on a fairly amateurish basis, i.e. putting food out and setting and checking traps. Certainly two of the squirrels remained in the wood for some time and were occasionally trapped. One of the squirrels was later spotted moving along a hedgerow some two miles from the release site and I knew this squirrel remained in the vicinity of a garden where it was regularly seen feeding over a period of eighteen months. However, when I set a trap in the wood one year later I was trapping and seeing grey squirrels only.

Peter Dickinson at the Welsh Mountain Zoo had one surviving male red squirrel from Scotland, so he requested a female. I was pleased to meet this request and as soon as the female arrived the male showed interest and breeding promptly occurred. When a second female was donated a significant breeding group was established. Peter Dickinson set up a stud book and a small group of captive breeders agreed to work collectively under Peter's leadership. In this way a reservoir of squirrels could be set up so that there would be a significant provision for any future release, as agreed and facilitated by English Nature. There are significant hazards to be overcome in captive breeding, especially coccidiosis and the parapox virus, which are usually fatal. High density may also lead to stress, which can end in fatal shock.

Quarantine laws regarding rabies have now been relaxed, with the result that a considerable number of red squirrels from Europe have been brought in to be sold by dealers. The price to my knowledge has ranged from £300 to £800 a pair. This has complicated the captive breeding scene, but may prove to be advantageous in time. Many British red squirrels seem to be distinctive in having a light champagne-coloured tail in summer but they readily breed with continental stock, and the study by V.P. Lowe and A.S. Gardiner, 'Is the British Squirrel British?' *(Mammal Review* 1983) states, 'Most squirrels in the British Isles appear to be variable in colour.' The specific aim of the study was to discover if British red squirrels possessed a distinctive skull shape. The conclusion was that the skull shapes of British and Continental reds were indistinguishable.

Skins were also studied and the paper suggested that there may have been a British race of red squirrel at one time, but it was already local, if not rare, by the eighteenth century. Certainly many squirrels were imported as pets in the eighteenth and nineteenth centuries. (I once possessed a Victorian cigarette card that showed a pet red squirrel sitting on top of an indoor cage, and the notes indicated that they could be bought in Leadenhall market.) Some of these escaped or were released and probably bred with native squirrels. Specific introductions were certainly known and recorded.

In looking at the skins the study found that only in the Spey Valley and certain areas in eastern Scotland, Thetford and Ireland were most squirrels found to have light tails in summer. There was translocation of squirrels within Britain as well as imports and the study suggested that light-tailed species may well have been sought after as an attractive variety.

One of my light-tailed squirrels had clear racoon-like rings throughout its tail in late summer and would undoubtedly have been highly prized by landowners seeking interesting colour morphs. Colour has certainly been a significant ingredient in the recent trade in red squirrels from Europe, as can be deduced from adverts and from the comments of dealers.

33

Racoon-like rings on the tail of a Northumbrian squirrel

In 1998 Kevin Hart, the Countryside Ranger at Kelling Holiday Park, approached me with a view to having some red squirrels for display and educational purposes. I visited Kelling intending to refuse his request, but when I saw the proposed enclosure and heard his outline of intention I was completely won over and most impressed with the educational aspects of his proposal. I described how the enclosure needed to be set up and was astonished three days later when he phoned to say my suggestions had been carried out.

His large enclosure was suitable for one male and two females and breeding promptly took place. One happy side issue happened to be quite accidental. The small enclosure adjoining the squirrels' cage houses two barn owls and this has had the effect of discouraging rats and mice, which can be a menace. Working closely with Kevin has proved a real benefit and helped to form the basis of an East Anglian squirrel group.

A grizzled elderly red with a bright copper juvenile, showing how colour varies with age. *Photo: Martin Hayward Smith*

5. Grey Squirrels and Red Herrings

On a holiday to Cromer in 1964 I caught the early morning bus to Sheringham and shared a seat with a forester. I asked him where in the Sheringham woods I might be able to see red squirrels. He told me there were no red squirrels in Norfolk, but greys would be seen in the late autumn. In fact, at that time there were no greys in North Norfolk and reds were fairly widespread. He was misled by the grey hairs on the coat of the red squirrel in autumn and, not having actually seen greys, he didn't realise that they don't grow ear tufts at all, whereas red squirrels do grow them in autumn as part of their winter coat. The seasonal changes in the coats of the two species can cause confusion, particularly in certain individuals. To add to this confusion the summer coat of the grey squirrel is often red-brown in colour. A well-known naturalist once summoned me to Norwich with the lure of a nest of four young squirrel kittens that had been rescued from their drey when the tree was felled. When I arrived to collect my prize my face must have shown the disappointment I felt when I saw them as he asked, 'What's the matter, they're not grey, are they?' This instance is typical of many occasions when someone has pointed out a 'red squirrel' to me when it was in fact a reddish-coloured grey.

A grey squirrel in brownish summer coat, killed on the road. It is most easily distinguished from the red by the white hairs fringing the tail

I was strolling through Regent's Park one morning on my way to the zoo when a father, walking with his two young children, drew their attention to a grey squirrel with a fairly yellow coat. He soon had a small crowd of about thirty people around him all admiring this 'red squirrel' as he called it. 'And you don't see many of those nowadays,' he added. I decided not to point out the error as it was clear that everyone else was quite convinced that what he said was correct. The last recorded sighting of a red squirrel in Regent's Park was in 1942, apart from the controlled release of ten from the zoo in 1986. On various occasions I have witnessed similar incidents in town parks, grey squirrels being mistaken for red.

I returned from a weekend away recently and was informed by a neighbour that a squirrel had been stunned by a car being driven down the road near my home. The people in the car called on my neighbour who directed them to me, but finding I was away, drove to the local vet and handed the squirrel over to the receptionist, insisting that it was a red squirrel. I phoned the vet the next day to make enquiries and found that the squirrel had died, but I was welcome to look at the body. When the receptionist brought it to me in a box she asked, 'Is it red or grey?' Sure enough the coat on the head and flanks was quite brown and I photographed the squirrel against the background of grey tarmac to use in my slide lectures. Nevertheless it was a grey. The best guide is to look at the outer fringe of hair on the tail. This is clearly grey in the grey squirrel. Also the shape of the animal is quite chunky compared to the slimline red.

On my 1975 family holiday in Cornwall we were walking up a chine to visit a waterfall. The chine was well wooded and there was a tea shop halfway up surrounded by trees. We stopped there for tea and I asked the proprietor if he had seen any red squirrels in the woodland as there were still isolated pockets of reds in Cornwall at that time. To my surprise he said readily, 'Oh, yes, they visit our bird table every day'. While I was drinking my tea he came and tapped me on the shoulder and whispered, 'There's one on the roof now.' I hurried outside and there it was, a grey! I duly photographed it on the roof so that I could use the slide as an example. I always follow up 'sightings' and I would think these occasions number over fifty in the course of the years and never has any claim proved to be positive.

It is worth mentioning at this point that there are grey squirrels that are black. There are some to be found at Letchworth and I have seen them in the grounds of Blenheim Palace in Oxfordshire. Also there are grey squirrels that are white. They occur in significant numbers in Kent. An injured white (grey) squirrel was taken to a vet in Kent and I was subsequently offered it. When I asked if it was red or grey, the vet replied with a degree of exasperation in her voice, 'It's white!' I went on to explain that it could be the white phase of the grey *(carolinensis)* or it might be a red *(vulgaris)*. It proved to be an albino grey. Incidentally the red and grey do not interbreed, though the colour variants of both species certainly once misled me to suspect this might be so. In my early teens I saw a grey in south London that had so much red on its coat I felt convinced it must have been a cross-breed and I followed it for some distance out of interest. Over the years several dozen observers have categorically stated to me that they have seen a half-breed red-grey.

In central Europe there are red squirrels that are black (melanic) and albino reds also occur, though less frequently. The latter are particularly attractive in appearance and some have recently been imported into this country and sold for considerable sums of money. Interestingly, black-greys are black all over and black-reds have a distinctive white belly.

The famous naturalist Frances Pitt, who used to write a column for the *London Evening News,* owned an albino red squirrel that had been found as an orphan and reared by hand. She named it 'Mrs Nuts' and it was the central character in her delightful little book published in 1954 entitled *My Squirrels.* The squirrels were all tame and lived in her house where they were allowed to roam free. In such circumstances toilets can be hazardous areas for squirrels, because they do have a keen thirst for water and a rather magnificent German orphaned male of hers ended up drowned in the cistern.

Since arriving in Norfolk I have had the good fortune to be in close touch with four zoology students studying the Thetford Forest squirrels, Jonathan Reynolds, Mike Jordan, Tim Venning and Janie Steele. It was during Jonathan Reynolds' studies in the early eighties that the greys were moving in and I remember him relating how he briefly left his tamed orphan red squirrel in the charge of friends and how on his return he found someone had left the toilet door open and there was the drowned squirrel in the toilet bowl. To lose a close companion in such circumstances must be heartbreaking. Each of the squirrels I have had in my keeping over the years has its own personality and it never ceases to be a wrench when they die, even in normal circumstances such as old age. (Jonathan Reynolds' study of the red squirrel's replacement by the grey squirrel in Eastern England was published in the *Journal of Animal Ecology* in 1985.)

6. Interaction?

Most naturalists deny any interaction between the two species. I am less sure. I believe it does take place, but it is certainly not the major reason for the replacement. However, there are some events I need to refer to.

When I lived in Barnet, North London, the enclosure I constructed for the squirrels had chicken wire within the wooden frame. It began to corrode after several years. One morning when I went to feed the squirrels I noticed that a grey had made entry into the enclosure. That in itself was an aggressive act as it was entering the reds' territory. This seemed an excellent opportunity to observe the relative behaviour of the two species. I watched what took place for approximately fifteen minutes. The reds seemed fairly unconcerned at first, but I noticed that the grey was very territorial and got increasingly aggressive, by rushing at the reds and leaping at them. They appeared to be more nimble in movement and were able to avoid contact, but as the interaction continued it became obvious that the reds were becoming exhausted and physical contact was being made. I allowed it to get to the point where I became alarmed for the safety of the reds and I felt I had to intervene. I was surprised to find that the grey was female. Perhaps this was significant, because it was lactating, which could have been the reason for its aggressive behaviour.

The grey squirrel is well camouflaged in birch woods

Photo: Martin Hayward Smith

When I lived in Worcestershire there were two other occasions when I witnessed interaction between red and grey. On these occasions there

A black (melanic) red squirrel feeding with an ordinary red at the reserve in Tilgate, Sussex

Photo given to the author

was solid wire between the two, but in both incidents the grey approached on top of the nearby fence, leapt on top of the enclosure and began sniffing at the reds below. On both occasions one of the reds leapt upside down on the wire and sniffed in return. The grey reacted by scrabbling at the wire and its posture was undoubtedly aggressive, so much so that I chased it off immediately and didn't wait to observe any more.

Kevin Hart, formerly Countryside Manager of the Holiday Park at Kelling, who works with me on the breeding project, observed an occasion when a grey came and perched in a pine tree adjoining the reds' enclosure and he said the reds immediately bolted for cover. (Fortunately Kevin, who has now become Centre Manager at Whitwell Hall, will keep his connection with Kelling as a consultant.)

There have been two occasions since I came to Fakenham when something drastic, possibly a virus, killed off several of my reds in a few days, and on both occasions a grey was spotted in my garden. On the first occasion one came right up to the window and my daughter drew my attention to it and on the second occasion the squirrel was killed crossing the road nearby. Resultant post mortems of the reds proved inconclusive. I just wonder when naturalists make apparently authoritative statements how detailed their personal observations are.

It is generally acknowledged that there are significant interactions between squirrels of the same species. If a number are kept together there is a clear hierarchical structure with dominant and subordinates and if newcomers are brought in great care needs to be taken, especially with males that are in breeding condition. I have been rash enough to try this with reds and a furious chase ensued with the two male squirrels locked in a vicious embrace. They were so firmly attached I had to knock them apart.

Kevin Hart has a stuffed grey squirrel for display purposes and when I asked him where he obtained it he said he saw it killed by another grey which leapt on it and bit it fatally on the back of the neck.

Douglas Middleton, in 1931, did record several eyewitness accounts of grey/red interaction during the changeover of the two species in southern England. Several combats were witnessed in Hertfordshire and on one occasion, after driving off the grey, a red squirrel was found dying from throat wounds. Similar incidents were reported from Kent and Somerset. Greys are known to be omnivorous and Middleton records that a grey was seen eating young red squirrels and that dead reds were found under dreys containing the American species. At Whipsnade in 1946, a grey was seen entering a red's drey and the two objects it dropped to the ground were retrieved and found to be young red squirrels bitten in the neck. A similar report from Cheshire recorded the death of three young reds. Middleton writes: 'Many accounts tell of

40

red squirrels being chased by greys, the pursued animal sometimes screaming as it raced along the branches.'

The red weighs in at around 300 grams as an adult whereas the grey can range between 510 and 750 grams. The average length of a red is 380 mm and a grey 475 mm. Thus the grey is larger and heavier than the red. It is quicker on the ground but the red has the edge in the trees and because it is lighter it is more nimble and can reach the cones in the high tops of the pines more easily. In a straight fight, if it came to that, it would be no contest, and certainly the grey in this country seems to have a more aggressive nature. It has been seen to despatch cockerels and sitting birds and observed to fight and kill rats, rabbits, leverets and even as powerful a predator as a stoat. I have known cats to come off worse in a scrap though I also know of cats that are very efficient predators of grey squirrels.

This evidence cannot lightly be dismissed, but there is also evidence of both species feeding apparently amiably near each other. Of the ten red squirrels released into Regent's Park in 1984 six were known road casualties, one known to have been killed by a cat, one disappeared without trace and the remaining two were not monitored after the time allowed for study. I do wonder about the road casualties - was a niche not available for them in the Park so that they were forced to seek pastures new and thus got run over? Road casualties are usually a sign of high numbers, but this would not be so in this case as there were only ten released.

Of course grey squirrels are also run over but not in excess of 60% of their numbers. In Regent's Park this would have totalled over 90 since it was estimated there were 150 greys resident at the time. During the study period of 20 months there were aggressive interactions between reds and greys and nearly 1500 were observed. When adult greys were involved 80% of these en-counters were won by greys and these mainly occurred during mating and dispersal seasons. Reasons given for the reds not being able to re-establish themselves in Regent's Park were high mortality and lack of reproduction to compensate.

The red squirrels did not breed, but they were less than a year old in 1985 and by 1986 the remaining animals were widely scattered and some interference by grey squirrels when female reds were *in œstrus* was noted and might have been a contributory factor. One personal observation at this point might be relevant. I was given two female red squirrels from Northumberland one autumn, and the older of the two produced a litter the following spring. I should have received two juveniles, but one was not available so I was given a mature female instead. It does raise the possibility that had the Regent's Park red squirrels been older, the breeding result might have been more positive.

In the Regent's Park interactions, although the red squirrel was not injured or driven far away, it was usually displaced from its position and would not have benefited from the interaction. Therefore they would be less able to relax, more hungry and more vulnerable to mortality agents.

The grey squirrels in the Regent's Park study obtained a significant proportion of their food from human activities (up to 30%) either directly or from litter bins. These food sources are points that less powerful individuals, i.e. red squirrels, could easily be excluded from. Also both are situated at ground level where greys are more at home. My captive reds have a distinct preference for being fed at human head height. The population densities of the two species seemed to affect the frequency of interactions between them.

The Woburn release of ten grey squirrels in 1890 and the Regent's Park release of ten red Squirrels in 1984 are an interesting parallel and a fascinating comparison. The result at Woburn of the release of the grey squirrels was such an overwhelming success that at least ten translocations of the progeny took place, all of which were in turn successful, including the one release of grey squirrels in Ireland at Castle Forbes.

Almost one hundred years later in 1984 ten red squirrels were released in Regent's Park into a grey squirrel area. Result: failure, at least from the point of view of re-establishment, though a great deal was learned in the process.

So how has the grey done it? The contention that it simply out-competes the red for food, I believe, is too facile. In some areas where the red has disappeared after the arrival of the grey, such as Wells pine woods in Norfolk, there was demonstrably more than enough food for both species, notably plentiful cones favoured by the red. My feeling is that the explanation is more subtle in that either a stress disease such as coccidiosis breaks out when there is a large squirrel population of either species or both, or dramatic as in the case of the parapox virus, which is deadly to the red and to which the grey is immune.

Grey squirrels seem to thrive happily in a higher density than red in deciduous woodland. John Gurnell, in the Mammal Society booklet *The Red Squirrel,* lists this as 1 red to 2 hectares and 5 or 6 greys to 2 hectares. That would certainly be a stress factor for red squirrels if 6 greys were present in the same territory. As John states: 'Red squirrels have never returned to broadleaf forest once grey squirrels have moved in and replaced them.' Coniferous forest shows a different picture. John Gurnell lists reds as 1 animal per 1 hectare and a similar figure for greys.

Other factors that tilt the balance in favour of grey in deciduous woodland are that they eat hard nuts earlier, before they are ripe, whereas reds wait until they are ripe by which time there may well be none left. Studies have shown that reds cannot remove the toxins in acorns as well as greys, causing digestive problems and weight loss if

42

This red squirrel blends in very well with a Scots pine trunk

Photo given to the author

their diet is predominantly acorns. The grey's ability to remove polyphenols in acorns, which are digestive inhibitors and toxins, gives them a competitive advantage in oak woods. Oaks form only 2% of Scottish woodland, which could be slowing the advance of greys in the north. Red squirrels put on about 10% of their body-weight at the onset of winter whereas greys increase their body-weight by at least 20%. Therefore in a lean spell and in competition with greys, reds are less likely to survive.

In cases where the disappearance of the red squirrel has been dramatic, particularly in coniferous areas where the red squirrel should be able to maintain its place, I believe the parapox virus seems to have been the determining factor. It appears that grey squirrels have the same response to parapox virus as sheep have to foot-and-mouth virus. Their immune response clamps down on the infection before they get sick and die whereas reds do not have this immune response to clamp down on the virus replication. If they do pass it on as carriers, it would seem likely that it persists on their bodies or they excrete it at a low level and that the reds catch it from them. Perhaps the grey squirrel flea, *Orchpaeas howardi*, which arrived from Armenia via its host, may also prove to be

43

an important factor, as it is found in grey dreys and reds and greys will enter each other's nests.

It springs to mind that there is an analogy with the Spanish conquistadors who took European diseases such as measles, smallpox and mumps to the New World while being immune themselves.

Undoubtedly the most significant factor in the disappearance of the red squirrels is the presence of the greys. Even laying aside the resultant disease factor, recent studies suggest that grey presence lowers juvenile red squirrel settlement and recruitment, which leads to a dwindling population in the longer term. Only in suitable habitat, i.e. coniferous forest, does it seem likely that the red squirrel can hold its own in the presence of grey.

Red squirrel summer drey

7. Vets and other Escapades

In the 1960s when I began keeping squirrels there were no RSPCA wildlife hospitals to turn to, so either I had to rely on instinct and common sense or the local vet. I constructed a small cage which I labelled 'hospital cage' and if a single squirrel fell sick I would quarantine it there and do what I could to get it fit again.

Over the years I have found that individual squirrels are prone to mites just as some humans are an attraction for horseflies while the insects completely ignore others. Evidently there is a certain squirrel mite, that it causes bare patches to appear on the squirrel in early spring. One of the two female squirrels I bought in 1964 was afflicted by mites, but I didn't realise what it was at the time, so I caught her up in a nest box and took her down to the local vet.

Fortunately I had the last appointment and I walked into the surgery armed with the nest box. The vet was an elderly grey-haired man who eyed the nest box apprehensively.

'What's in there?' he asked, eyes dilating.

'A red squirrel,' I replied.

'Does it bite?' he asked, sharply.

'Well, it hasn't yet,' I replied, a little uncertainly.

This must have been a disconcerting answer as I found out later that he had once been bitten by a grey squirrel.

'Right! I'll coax it out and you grab it!' he directed.

Thus he coaxed and I missed!

You may well picture the scene that followed, as the vet and I both bounded round the surgery after the fleeing squirrel, he with shouts of, 'Grab the towel! Grab the towel!' which, coupled with his peculiar accent and the general chaos of the melée, I interpreted as, 'Grab the tail! Grab the tail!' After a sharp and breathless altercation between us as to the merits and otherwise of such a course of action I finally realised he was shouting, 'Grab the towel' not tail, so I glanced round the surgery till I spied it. I snatched it and several times flung it in the direction of the squirrel as it rocketed round the surgery. Of course I missed but tried to improve my skill as a matador with each throw. After a period of general mayhem, which can be easily pictured, I was successful at last. Fortunately, as soon as its eyes were covered, the squirrel quietened down and I was able to hold it up for the vet's close inspection, while he fought to regain his breath and decide on a course of action.

He peered closely at the bare skin and clearly was unsure of the reason for it. This was understandable as he had not encountered it before and the mites cannot be spotted by the naked eye. It was years later, when Ian Robinson of the RSPCA Wildlife Hospital took a skin sample, that he discovered the mites on taking a close look through the microscope. On this occasion, however, the vet obviously felt he must give a show of firm action and he said, 'I think I'll give it a shot of penicillin!' This must have proved a shock to the system as I found the following day the squirrel was blind, and for the rest of its life it could only shuffle around, feeling its way.

The vet obviously thought that to complete the job he must follow this up, and his eyes roved round the surgery until they came to rest on a large jar of unlabelled yellow liquid. He poured some into an empty bottle and, after searching for some time, he managed to find a label. He rummaged through a drawer at his desk and pulled out a biro and studiously wrote something on the bottle. I assumed it would be the name of some special elixir, but I was too stunned by the experience to ask at the time. When I got home I unwrapped the bottle and there on the label was printed THREE TIMES A DAY. In due course of time there was a new growth of fur and the mites died off. I believe this was due to the life cycle of the mites rather than the all-purpose elixir!

Several years after this event, after successful breeding, two of my seven squirrels died suddenly and I decided to ask the assistance of a new vet. He asked me to bring the bodies to him immediately and sent them off for post mortem analysis. The result was a clear case of coccidiosis. The vet explained that there were coccidia in the gut but in times of considerable stress these would multiply and the animal's defence mechanism would not be able to cope.

Thus I realised that my enclosure could house a limited number of squirrels and to go above this number would cause stress and a crash in numbers. This vet also gave me some liquid in a bottle. It was dark brown in colour and he said if I put a few drops in the water it would deal with the coccidia if administered in time. This did in fact prove effective on two subsequent occasions.

Some years later, a photographer borrowed one of the squirrels to photograph. He had it for some time and phoned me one day to ask if he could return it as it was 'off colour.' I found that it could hardly get about and shuffled along, but outwardly looked healthy. I nursed it for a few days and kept it under close observation. Then I heard a persistent gnawing sound and I saw it was chewing at the breeze blocks I had used as supports for an internal shed within the enclosure. After consuming a sizeable amount together with its regular food it recovered completely and could leap and climb as well as ever. I can only conclude it had some mineral or calcium deficiency, and the food it had been given did not provide it with that necessary part of its diet. I have subsequently found that deer antlers are an excellent natural remedy for calcium deficiency and far preferable to breeze blocks!

After those initial experiences with sick squirrels I realised that I might as well deal with invalids as best I could in future, so I made my small 'hospital cage' and nursed a number of squirrels through coccidiosis and other minor ailments.

I made the mistake of lending out my breeding male to a residential school as an educational aid but they called me up one day to report it sick and 'please would I collect it'. When I did so I discovered they were feeding it on guinea pig food. This might have been satisfactory with grey squirrels as they are omnivorous, but reds seem more particular about their diet and the male squirrel had not thrived on the food provided. I received it at such a late stage I had no time to redress the situation and it died within hours.

· In the late 1980s the RSPCA Wildlife Hospital at East Winch opened and on several occasions they came to my rescue and very skilfully dealt with various ailments suffered by the squirrels. As my garden is surrounded by arable land, brown rats are a hazard in autumn when the crops are harvested. They seem to gain entrance under the wire via the old mole tunnels. They proved to be unpleasant bedfellows for the squirrels and occasionally behaved quite viciously. They were not easy to deal with because poisons could not be placed in the enclosures and they were quite trap-resistant. Trapping the rats was not an easy task anyway with the squirrels *in situ*. One tame squirrel I had been given was blind and unfortunately was bitten on the eye by a rat. I took her to East Winch RSPCA and they performed a remarkably successful operation and removed the injured eye. It healed beautifully and she

Deer antlers are a very good source of calcium
Photo: Martin Hayward Smith

47

survived very happily for over a year after that and died at the good age of seven years old.

At the time of writing, the hospital has just successfully dealt with a face abscess on one of the squirrels and it is well on the way to recovery after suffering a bite. In the wild, the animal would almost certainly die.

I had one Fakenham squirrel whose fur was attacked by mites. This was a female squirrel who had successfully reared twenty-eight young ones over a period of five years. In preparing her nursery nest she would use some tree bark and in doing so would scoop up some eggs of the mites and transfer them to the nest and in due course they transferred themselves to the squirrel. On one occasion I took the squirrel, named Feline, to East Winch and Ian Robinson, the vet in charge, took a scrape and later, under the microscope, he discovered the mites. With regular changes of bedding I was able to interrupt the life-cycle of the mites and after that the use of 'Head and Tail' powder kept the mites at bay. I have a friend in Canada who comments: 'We notice some squirrels in winter have large patches of bare skin', so clearly the occurrence is not limited to the U.K., or is this another unfortunate import?

In the spring of 2000 I had a 'phone call from Ian Keymer, an eminent retired vet who had worked for MAFF for many years and had done some crucial work on the parapox virus. He had received a report of a red squirrel, which had been visiting a bird-table in West Lynn for some days. He asked me what I made of the report and, as the description given seemed authentic, I immediately investigated and met Mrs Manning-Coe who lived in West Lynn. She showed me the willow tree in an adjoining garden where it could often be seen and also the blackbird's nest under the garage overhang where it had taken up temporary residence at night. Hospitably she offered me a cup of tea and I was shown a video of the squirrel that had been taken by her brother-in-law. At this point the squirrel, aptly named Cyril by the Manning-Coes, was spotted dozing in its customary place on the willow tree.

We promptly went outside and took a closer look. I could see it was a mature male with very long ear tufts and, by its appearance, just over 300 grams in weight. My guess was that it might have been a stowaway on the timber boats that regularly docked at Lynn or perhaps travelled in on one of the sugar-beet loads that regularly travelled between Lynn and Portugal. In any event it seemed unlikely that it would survive for long, despite its initiative in using the local facilities, that is, the bird-table goodies and the convenient shelter of the bird's nest. The local cats had already shown a considerable interest and their predatory instincts had been aroused. So I asked Mrs Manning-Coe if I could trap it and incorporate it into the captive breeding scheme. Three days later I had a call to say that Cyril was inside the nest box trap I had set and would I please come and collect. I quarantined him for a period before intro-

48

ducing him to a female squirrel and the following year two successful litters were reared from that pair.

We had a subsidiary group of four squirrels kept by a farmer in the Acle area. One autumn night, a number of rat-holes appeared and by morning three of the squirrels had been bitten and one escaped presumably through a rat-hole. We assumed it had also been bitten and would die within days like the other three, but to our amazement four months later, in spring, we found it had been regularly feeding on someone's bird-table, a mere three miles away. It had made its way via hedgerows to a small spinney and had set up home there with the bird-table nuts providing a regular food source. After some persuasion the owner of the bird-table allowed us to catch the squirrel, a female, and she is now back in the breeding group at Kelling, having provided one litter so far and doing very well.

Perhaps the individual lives of two other squirrels deserve some reference. The first, named Copper, gained immortality by providing the pelt from my 'Nutcase' that I use to recreate that pivotal moment in 1940 when the Infants teacher held up the red squirrel. Normally I bury the squirrels when they die, but Copper had such an adventurous life I felt she ought to have more lasting fame, so I kept her skin and, when appropriate, I refer to one or other of her escapades. Copper was something of an escapologist, but never permanently left the security of home, just had need for temporary adventure.

At 7 o'clock one morning I had a 'phone call from a neighbour to say that one my squirrels was in his weeping willow tree. I have built my enclosures round two apple trees and the upper branches poke out through the wire. In high winds this leads to some displacement of the wire and on this occasion Copper had squeezed out of the narrow aperture and decided to investigate the local gardens. By the time I was alerted she had already decided to make her way back, but when she reached the mature oak behind the enclosure she decided to rest and remain in the fork. I could not coax her down so I sectioned off her favourite part of the cage complex and left the door open, making sure the rest of the squirrels were separated in other sections. When I returned from school that evening Copper was safely tucked up in her nest box, none the worse for her adventure. A fortnight later she gave birth to a litter of three young, so perhaps her excursion was to consider an alternative nursery nest.

She obviously enjoyed the vantage point she had in the oak tree because she found her way out twice more and took up temporary residence there. As the oak tree seemed so popular I thought with a little ingenuity I could incorporate it into the enclosure and when I did just that, Copper's wanderlust ended.

However a further adventure awaited her. I was transferring her on loan to a colleague and, while I was moving the trap she was in, a predatory cat became over-interested. In trying to ward it off I over-tilted the trap and Copper was out and off into the nearest hedge in a flash. The hedgerow consisted of thick hawthorn in the dense foliage of mid-summer and searching for a squirrel in there was truly like looking for a needle in a haystack, so the search was soon abandoned. We thought that was our last sight of her, only to hear one week later that Alan Marrett of Aylmerton Field Study Centre had a red squirrel 'recovering' after being rescued from the jaws of his cat.

The centre was one mile away from where Copper had been last seen. Alan was returning to the Centre and when his vehicle swung in the entrance he saw the cat actually pounce on the squirrel - what timing! He leapt out and ran to the scene getting the cat to drop the squirrel with a little gentle persuasion. He then nursed the shocked squirrel back to a full recovery. Copper was duly returned to me and survived to retiring age!

Erica in winter coat

Another endearing character was Erica. She was an orphaned Lake District red squirrel that had been brought up by hand and offered to me to be incorporated into the breeding programme. She was given to me as a male called Eric (the Red). When she arrived it was apparent that she was female, so I had to rename her Erica. It was soon apparent that she had very little sight, if any, as she kept bumping into obstacles until she became thoroughly familiar with the surroundings. However, all her other faculties were excellent and although she clearly would have succumbed in the wild very quickly, in the sheltered environment of captivity she had a very satisfactory life and produced a litter of four daughters, which were incorporated into the national breeding programme.

Since I handled her food some of my scent would be on it and vice versa so Erica would occasionally test my skin out with her needle sharp teeth, on occasions drawing blood. Once, I was being interviewed on a Wildlife Rescue TV programme and, as I was endeavouring to give my views on why the red squirrel was in decline, Erica decided to test my fingers out causing a trickle of blood to flow neatly down in full view of the camera. This elicited a broad grin from me in mid-sentence, so a retake was required. I have always expected to see the clip on one of those 'wrong take' TV programmes, but if it is still in the can I haven't spied it yet.

8. Past, Present and Future

So what has been achieved since 1964? Well, first a vast number of people have had the opportunity to see a delightful animal at close quarters. A particular joy for me has been to share their expression of pleasure at seeing a red squirrel for the first time. One particular comment immediately springs to mind when a local High School teacher called to see a red and compare it with the many greys he was so familiar with. 'It's like comparing a Rolls-Royce with a Mini,' he said and of course he had beauty rather than size in mind.

With Peter Dickinson of Welsh Mountain Zoo at the helm and keeping the stud book, a significant network of captive breeders has been set up and various experiments, including monitored release, have been or are taking place with considerable support and backup from English Nature and PTES (People's Trust for Endangered Species). Also, in the spring of 2001 Mammals Trust UK was launched and the red squirrel was one of its target species.

There is a healthy population of red squirrels on the Isle of Wight, and the islands in Poole Harbour also have stable populations. Off the west coast of Scotland it is reassuring that the large island of Arran has many red squirrels and the efforts on Anglesey are paying dividends with reduced numbers of grey and increasing numbers of reds.

As far as the mainland is concerned the grey continues to advance and the red retreat. The replacement is so well established that increasing numbers of people believe the grey is the native species and the red the alien.

Grey squirrel control still continues regularly in many places when their destructive activities bite commercially, but the national concerted effort in the fifties was a failure. In six years, 1953-1958, one and a half million grey squirrels were shot and the bounty paid out on their tails was in excess of £100,000, but it became apparent that as one wood was virtually cleared, a vacuum was created that was almost immediately filled by squirrels from outside the area. The Rector of Wells told me that as a teenager he and a friend shot two hundred grey squirrels in four Surrey gardens in two days. This earned him some excellent pocket-money, but made no overall impact on local squirrel numbers and was indicative of a very large population. One Surrey market gardener in the 1950s shot two hundred and eighty-two grey squirrels in three months and still lost half his strawberry crop.

The inexorable march of the grey squirrel in Britain is the most successful invasion since 1066. Having set that train in motion in 1876 with the first introduction should we attempt to stop or slow the train down or let it take its own course and just accept the consequences? I have lost count of the number of people who love to see the grey squirrel on their bird-tables and some have mooted that we should just accept that the bigger animal is a natural supplanter of the native and let nature take its course. Of course, the Surrey market gardener, the Fakenham man who had a £300 bill as a result of grey squirrel damage, the Shropshire couple who returned from holiday to be faced with a £4,000 bill for squirrel-damage repairs, and scores of others with loft damage would take a different view.

The Timber Growers' Association recently described the grey squirrel as 'a very serious threat to forests and wildlife, especially song-birds'. It is particularly partial to the inner bark and sap of sycamore, beech, ash, oak, maple, horse chestnut, birch, lime, apple, cherry, and occasionally pine and larch, mainly during May, June and July. The bark-stripping often inflicts wounds that allow easy penetration by insects and fungi, which degrades timber quality.

At one time studies were taking place with a view to producing an effective birth pill for the grey squirrel. This, of course, received substantial opposition from those who oppose on principle and from those who feel its charm outweighs its wanton acts of destruction. As we move nearer to a full understanding of genetics, an amusing little rhyme, which appeared in a circular on squirrel data, is worthy of reflection:-

Mary had a little lamb, its fleece was slightly grey.
It didn't have a father, just some borrowed DNA.
It sort of had a mother, though its ovum was on loan.
It was not so much a lambkin, as a little lamby clone.
And soon it had a fellow clone, and soon it had some more.
They followed her to school one day, all cramming through the door.
It made the children laugh and sing, the teachers found it droll.
There were too many lamby clones for Mary to control.
No other could control the sheep since their programmes didn't vary.
So the scientists resolved it all, by simply cloning Mary.
But now they feel quite sheepish, those scientists unwary.
One problem solved, but what to do, with Mary, Mary, Mary...

Encouragingly the reds in the pines at Formby, on the Sefton coast, continue to flourish and the controlled releases in North Wales at the Welsh Mountain Zoo and at Tilgate in Sussex flourished for a significant period with successful breeding which led to a build-up in numbers before both groups succumbed to the dreaded parapox virus. In the case of Tilgate Nature Centre, Gary Clarke, the Curator, preferred to say the red squirrels became 'free range' by accident rather than intention, as one had been placed on a tree on an island and it promptly swam across the intervening water and on to the mainland. Others escaped from their enclosure, but re-appeared the following morning to seek food. At that point it was decided to leave them at large and see what happened. They remained under the management of the Centre, but would obviously benefit from supplementary feeding. Under these circumstances they bred, and their numbers built up to between ten and twenty until parapox virus caused the death of all but three; the disease caught up with even these three later and they all died. Although the virus won in both Formby and Tilgate, the experience gained was valuable and the search goes on for a satisfactory solution to this problem. The intriguing survival of red squirrels alongside greys in central Liverpool, in what would normally be regarded as poor deciduous habitat, is also a great encouragement.

Norfolk-bred red squirrels on view at Flamingo Park, Isle of Wight

Photo given to the author

In Cumbria there is an excellent initiative, suitably titled 'Red Alert - North West', which is leading a concerted effort to conserve the Lake District red squirrels as the greys advance and similar steps have been taken in the North-East with considerable interest and co-operation from Forestry Commission and private landowners. The logo of red alert was very eye-catching. It was the silhouette of a red squirrel sitting above a clock that is ticking towards 12 noon. In other words, time is short. A further venture of the Cumbrian Wildlife Trust was launched in 2002, called Friends of the Red Squirrel, Red Alert North West. Positive

54

evidence of awareness of the red squirrel's plight can also be seen at Oasis Whinfell Forest in Cumbria, which is an excellent example of a coniferous 'island' forest in an agricultural landscape; wardens there at Center Parcs are very aware of the heritage of red squirrels that the Forest holds. This is very encouraging as the grey squirrel is not likely to take over almost unnoticed there as has happened in most of England and Wales. Some landowners in the North are managing their woodlands as mini refuges for the red squirrel and creating such refuges is one of the stated aims of Red Alert North West.

In 1903 after a couple of years of exploring a southern swathe of the New Forest by bicycle, W. H. Hudson wrote his delightful monograph *Hampshire Days* which includes a poetic description of a sighting of a red squirrel. If our conservation efforts bear fruit, at least in some places on mainland Britain, people will have that unique joy of seeing the 'bright red squirrel in the mist and wet and soft airs in late November.'

In the light of the deadly nature of the parapox virus to red squirrels it is not feasible to release reds into East Anglia at the time of writing, so our captive breeding of reds has expanded to Weybourne Forest Lodges, Natural Surroundings, Letheringsett, and, particularly important, the Countryside section at Easton College where students are involved All these locations have the educational aspect of the project very much at

**Red squirrel between the viewing panels at Flamingo Park,
Isle of Wight**

Photo given to the author

heart, but they also keep a toehold here while we buy time. Close connections are also maintained with Pensthorpe Waterfowl Park and Banham Zoo.

The recent paper on the virus published by the Royal Society (Tompkins, Sainsbury, Nettleton, Buxton, Gurnell), proving that the virus is highly pathogenic in the red squirrel while having no detectable effect on the grey, also suggests that the development of a red squirrel vaccine against parapox virus has a good chance of conferring a high degree of immunity to the disease; this gives cause for hope.

There is encouragement also from successful breeding at Dudley Zoo, Paradise Park in Cornwall and Bolton, Lancashire, in 2002, and from the fact that viewers of the TV programme, 'Bill Oddie goes Wild', put the red squirrel at the top of their list of animals they wished to see in the British countryside.

An excellent example of an informative set-up is at Flamingo Park Wildlife Encounter, Seaview, Isle of Wight. Three of our Norfolk captive-bred squirrels were transferred there in July 2001. Visitors to the Park can view the squirrels through glass panels in the information room as well as from the outside of the enclosure, ensuring that they are able to see red squirrels even if they do not spot them in the wild.

Optimistically and determinedly Janie Steele, who was the last guardian of the Thetford reds, said to me in her attractive Scottish burr:

'We won't give up on the red squirrels, David, will we?'

We certainly won't. It's a battle worth winning.

❀❀❀❀❀

Appendix: Greys in Essex

An article by Stephen Harris in the Essex Naturalist 1973/4 entitled 'History and Distribution of Squirrels in Essex' is particularly helpful in providing a picture of the advance of greys and retreat of reds in East Anglia. The maps included show the grey moving in from the west, and the red melting away to the east. His general comment on the years 1945-70 was, 'During this twenty-five year period the red squirrel declined from being an animal that was common throughout the county to one on the verge of extinction'. Nevertheless the disappearance was not always swift. For instance, he writes, 'the last red squirrel was seen in Epping Forest a quarter of a century after the appearance of the first greys'.

A recent letter from an Essex resident to an East Anglian Journal contributes the following:

'When I came to live in a village in north Essex in 1959, I was surprised to find that there were still red squirrels there, since they had already long since disappeared from the neighbourhood of my home in Wiltshire. That summer, however, the first grey squirrels were seen. On November 20th, 1961 I wrote in my natural history diary:

"The family of red squirrels – three or four of them – which inhabit the oak trees in front of our house, and the larches beyond, have already acquired their winter coats. Only a week ago they were quite red, but now their backs and flanks and tails are of a beautiful mauvish-grey and their coats are much longer – tails now very full and eartufts long. They are delightful animals and spend most of their time playing hide and seek with each other – very entertaining to watch."

That was the last entry which recorded a sighting of red squirrels. They retired to their dreys when the weather turned very cold in December, but the following spring they failed to reappear.'

This letter went on to ask why? I believe it likely that the parapox virus was to blame, in which case the end would have been swift. The non-emergence would not have been due to cold weather, as squirrels can be seen foraging in the coldest temperatures and seem to prefer this to wind and rain; neither reds nor greys hibernate as old text books used to claim.

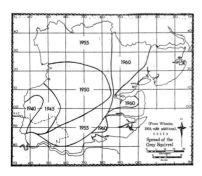

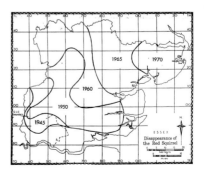

Red squirrels in conference. Can they survive?
Photo: Martin Hayward Smith

RED SHRINKS FROM GREY

Like the last ember
In a swamp of cold morning-after ashes,

Like the tail light
Of a sprightly old lady's bicycle
Losing her slowly in the fog.

Stuart Medland